CATS
CLOSE UP

Devon Rex

Howard Loxton

Newborn kitten

Playful kittens

Caracal

Persian cat

Cats
Close Up

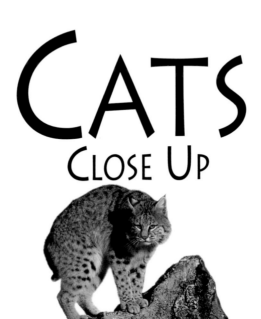

Bobcat

SILVERDALE BOOKS

Produced by
Elm Grove Books Limited
Series Editor Susie Elwes
Text Editor Angela Wilkes
Art Director Louise Morley
Picture research Joanne Beardwell
Illustration John Woodcock
Index Hilary Bird
Original Edition © 2000
Image Quest Limited
This edition © 2002

Elm Grove Books Limited

Text and Photographs in this book
previously published in
Eyewitness 3D Cats

Published by
SILVERDALE BOOKS
an imprint of Bookmart Ltd
Registered Number 2372865
Trading as Bookmart Ltd
Desford Road
Enderby
Leicester LE9 5AD

ISBN 185605695-3

A C.I.P. Catalogue record for this title is
available from the British Library.

Printed by Dai Nippon
Printing Company
HongKong

ACKNOWLEDGMENTS
Photography
Heather Angel: 3BR, 5BR, 9L, 19TR, 21TL, 45L, 51BCL; **Ardea:**Francoise Gonnier 15BC/Charles McDougal 25BR/Stephan Meyers 37BR; **Robert Bloomberg:** 6, 7TR, 10, 11TR, 20, 21TR, 28, 29TR; **BBC**/Ingo Bartussek 43CR/Peter Blackwell 47TC,/Simon King 13TL/Owen Newman 25TL, /Dietmar Nill 33TL/Anup Shah 47TC/Lynn Stone 41BC; **Christies Images** 15TL; **Bruce Coleman**/Adriano Bacchella 17L/E&P Bauer 43L, 49BC, 51BR/Jane Burton 5TL, 23BR, 29Bl, 33Bl, 45TC, 49BR, 54R, 58L /Alain compost 11CR/Gerald Cubitt 53C/HPH Photography 13 BR, 54R, 58L/Johnny Johnson 51BL/Steve Kaufman 1BL, 19C/Werner Layer 25BC/Joe McDonald 37TL/Luiz Claudio Marigo 7TL/Rita Meyer 15BL/Dr Eckart Pott 7BC, 31BC/Hans Reinhard 1CR/John Shaw 7BL/Rod Williams 11TL, 27BR, 39R, 53TC, 53R/Gunter Ziesler 37TR, 53L/Jean-Pierre Zwaenepoel 26, 27TR/**Inc**/Tom Brakefield 11R; **Frank Greenaway**/NHM 5TR; **Frank Lane Photo Agency**/Tony Hamblin 13TC/Gerald Lacz 5BL, 17TC,19L, 47Bl, 47BR, 56L/ W Wisniewski 45BC /MB Withers 21BCR; **NHPA**/Anthony Bannister 9CR/Susanne Danegger 37BL/Nigel Dennis 2TC/Daniel Heuclin 31TC, /Kitchin & Hurst 5TC/Gerard Lacz 17, 58BR /Yves Lanceau 17R/Kevin Schafer 21BCL; **Oxford Scientific Films**/Lon Lauber 23BL/Stan Osolinski 29BR/Richard Packwood 41TC, 50, 51TR/Hans Reinhard 27BL,/Marty Stouffer 42, 43TR; **Planet Earth**/Steve Bloom 13Bl/Tom Brakefield 12, 13TR/Alain Dragesco 7BR/Carol Farneti-Foster 8, 9TR, 23TC/Robert Franz 9CL, 54L/M&C Denis-Huot 43BL, 48, 49TR/Brian Kenney 21BL/P Kumar 39L /Ken Lucas 11Cl/ Lythgoe 39CL/Anup Shah 21BR, 32, 33TR, 41L; **Science Photo Library**/Cath Wadforth/Hull University 29TR; **Tony Stone Images**/Tim Davis 34, 35TR/Art Wolfe 31BL; **Warren Photographic** /Jane Burton &Kim Taylor: 1Tl, 1TC, 1BR, 3T, 4, 15TC, 15TR, 15BR, 16, 17TR, 18, 19TC, 22, 23TR, 25BL, 27TL, 27TC, 31BR, 33TC, 33BR, 38, 39TR, 39CR, 40, 41TR, 45BR, 47TL, 49BL, 52, 53TR, 56R: **Windrush Photos**/David Tipling 41BR.

CONTENTS

Anxious kitten

Lynx

MOTHER AND KITTEN
All cats are mammals. The kittens or cubs grow inside their mother and are born live. They feed on their mother's milk and are cared for until they are old enough to hunt.

THE CAT FAMILY

All cats are descended from an animal called Pseudaelurus, which lived 20 million years ago. The last of the ancient group of saber-toothed cats, Smilodon, died out 10,000 years ago, victims of the changing climate. Other cat groups adapted more successfully. These cats were slimmer and faster than the saber-tooths. Their teeth were highly specialized so they could kill their prey quickly. The effortless grace and hunting skill of cats make them rewarding animals to study.

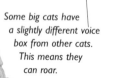

Some big cats have a slightly different voice box from other cats. This means they can roar.

CAT SKELETON
All members of the cat family have a very similar skeleton with exactly the same bones. A speedy cheetah's legs are no longer proportionally than those of other cats, but their bones are lighter.

LYNX

The lynx belongs to a group of cats called wildcats. The European lynx is threatened with rapid extinction. It is the largest cat species found in Europe: five times heavier than a pet cat.

The sharp edge of the saber-tooth is at the back.

Specialized, conical canine teeth

EXTINCT SABER-TOOTH

Saber-toothed cats had large canine teeth like daggers. They killed their prey by taking a huge bite from the fleshy part of an animal. The sharp backward-slicing blades of the top teeth savagely tore out a chunk of flesh and tough hide. Saber-tooths and their prey are now extinct.

JAGUAR FANGS

Modern cats have conical-shaped canine teeth that thrust between the bones on the neck of their prey and cut the spinal cord. To kill very large animals, cats bite their throats or muzzles and suffocate them. Modern cats are fast and athletic: qualities they developed following an increase in the numbers of fast prey that grazed a new world of grassy plains.

The spotted cat has a similar coat pattern to its larger cousins.

THE SMALL CATS

All the cat groups contain some small cats. The ocelot group are mostly small cats and almost all are found in the Americas. Some of these cats live in forests, like their ancestors; others live on the pampas (plains) or in the mountains. Small cats in the pantherine group include the leopard cat and the smaller African black-footed cat. Domestic cats belong to a third group: the wildcats. Domestic cats often live together, but their wild relatives have solitary lives.

LITTLE SPOTTED CAT

The little spotted cat is a member of the ocelot family. It is highly endangered because it is hunted for its attractive coat. The rain forest, where the spotted cat lives in Central and South America, is rapidly disappearing.

OCELOT

The ocelot is found in forests and scrubland from Arizona to Argentina. Ocelots often live in pairs and hunt by day. They have been extensively killed for their beautiful fur coats.

BIG EARS

The serval has proportionally the largest ears of any cat, which it uses to listen for under-ground prey. It roams grassy plains in many parts of Africa. It climbs well and often catches birds, leaping 3 m (10 ft) into the air.

DESERT HOME

The sand cat lives in the deserts of North Africa and Arabia. It is about 50 cm (20 in) long. It hides in scrub or in underground burrows to shelter from the heat of the day. It survives on little water, obtaining enough liquid from the blood of its prey.

Bobcat coats range from pale fur with pale spots to black spots and dark fur.

AMERICAN BOB

Bobcats live throughout North America in terrain ranging from rocky mountain and brushland to swampy tropical forest. In the 1970s, 92,000 bobcats were killed yearly. The Mexican bobcat is now an endangered species.

Long fur protects the sand cat's paws from the hot sand.

THE BIG CATS

The tiger's stripes make it easy to distinguish from the other big cats.

Among the most successful predators on land are the eight different big cats: tigers, lions, leopards, cheetahs, pumas or cougars, jaguars, snow leopards, and clouded leopards. They are all closely related and belong to the pantherine group of cats. They are covered in variety of patterns and share a glorious, athletic grace. Big cats began to flourish three million years ago as the saber-toothed cat started to die out.

MIGHTY TIGER
Tigers are the largest of all the cats. The biggest, the Siberian tiger, is about 4 m (13ft) long. Tigers live mainly in forests from Siberia south to India and Sumatra. Several species are extinct and the rest are highly endangered.

PROWLING LEOPARD
The leopard lives on scrub and grassland in Africa and Southeast Asia, but it regularly climbs trees. It likes wet areas but can adapt to a wide range of habitats. This makes it the most successful survivor among the big cats.

JAGUARS
Jaguars are the largest of the American cats. Hundreds of thousands have been killed for their fur coats. They are extinct in Arizona, Mexico, and south of Brazil.

SNOW LEOPARD
The snow leopard lives alone in the high snow-covered mountains of Central Asia above 3,000 m (10,000 ft). Smaller than the leopard, its beautiful coat makes it a target for poachers.

LIONESS
Lions live in central Africa, Kruger National Park in South Africa, and in the Gir Forest in India. An adult lion is about 3 m (10 ft) long and has a shaggy mane and tufted tail. Females are smaller.

9

ODD CATS

Cats are so similar that the different species can interbreed. In captivity, tigers and lions have produced tiglon and liger cubs. Leopards and pumas have also produced young together. The small differences between cats are often a specialization for hunting or living in a particular environment. Some differences affect a cat's appearance and others their performance, such as a cheetah's speed or a puma's mighty leaps.

JAGUARUNDI

Adult jaguarundi look like large weasels. They have a slender body, short legs, a long tail, and a small head. Their kittens look more catlike. Jaguarundi live in lowland forest and bush from Central America to Uruguay.

Low-set ears and cheek ruffs make the head look wide.

PALLAS' CAT

This Asian cat hunts among rocks for its prey. Its eyes are near the top of its face so when it peers over a rock it shows only the top of its head.

CLOUDED LEOPARD

The clouded leopard lives in the forests of Southeast Asia, although it is rarely seen in the wild. It is highly acrobatic in trees. This small leopard can climb while hanging upside down, run headfirst down a tree trunk, and leap 5 m (16 ft) between trees.

The tail of the clouded leopard is as long as its body.

KING CHEETAH

A king cheetah runs as fast as other cheetahs, but unlike them its spots are large and joined together in stripes along its spine. King cheetahs may grow a little larger than other cheetahs.

Paws conceal unusually blunt claws.

FLAT-HEADED CAT

The small flat-headed cat has a long body and short legs. It is rare and is thought to live by rivers from India to Indonesia.

Hard, pointed toes and blunt claws boost running speeds.

QUICK CAT

The cheetah is not only the fastest cat: it is also the fastest animal on land. Cheetahs sprint at speeds up to 96 kph (60 mph). They were once widespread, but now live mainly on the African plains, where they use their speed to hunt antelope and gazelle. They are different from the other big cats since they have a small head and a slender body. They hunt by daylight but take care to avoid lions.

CHEETAHS AT COURT
In the sixteenth century the Indian Emperor Akbar kept 3,000 cheetahs, which he used for hunting. The last wild cheetah living in India was seen in 1956.

The tail acts to balance the swift movements of the cheetah's body.

RACING CAT
Cheetahs run at high speed for 400-600 m (440-660 yd), and at this speed can alter course if their prey changes direction.

The bending and straightening of a cheetah's flexible spine adds about 76 cm (30 in) to the length of its stride.

EXHAUSTED CHEETAH

A high-speed chase exhausts a cheetah, which will rest for 30 minutes or so before it can sprint again or eat its kill. Even when they have recovered, cheetahs are often driven away from their kill by lions or packs of hyenas.

The mother raises her paw to bat the gazelle and prevent it from escaping.

ROLE MODEL

A cheetah cub learns how to hunt from its mother, watching how she bats a gazelle to the ground and bites its throat. As cubs grow older, a mother cheetah encourages the cubs to practice killing small gazelles for themselves.

KEEPING COMPANY

Not all male cheetahs live alone. Cheetahs from the same litter often stay together, or join up with other males in groups of two or three. Adult females, however, usually live alone, unless they are rearing cubs.

Earrings adorn this Egyptian statue of a cat.

MOVING INDOORS

Stores of grain attract rodents, and a plentiful supply of rats and mice attracts cats. This is probably the reason cats began hunting inside. The first record of domesticated cats comes from Egyptian wall paintings, which are 3,750 years old. The domestic cat later spread from Egypt throughout the Roman empire. In India, China, and Japan, domestic cats were also kept to keep rodents from damaging grain stores, silk cocoons, and temple manuscripts.

EGYPTIAN SCULPTURE
The Egyptian goddess Bast was often shown as a cat. Cats in Egypt were revered. When they died cats were embalmed and buried in cemeteries reserved for them.

AFRICAN WILDCAT
The African wildcat was the species domesticated by the Egyptians. They are pictured as hunting cats that help to kill wild fowl. Cats in Egypt were treated as members of the family.

CAT COMFORTS

Few modern cats have to catch rats and mice. Like other pets they enjoy our love and attention, food, and their own space.

MOUSE AT HOME?

A cat's eyes dilate to see into the dark mouse hole. Its whiskers bend forward to "feel" for any movement within the hole. The cat listens for tiny noises, and may wait to ambush the emerging mouse.

CAT SHOW

A lot of work goes into preparing a cat for the show ring. Cat breeders enter their pets for the best of breed prizes and for the prize of show champion.

Cats prefer a harness to a collar when on a leash.

CAT LEASH

Some cats walk on a leash like a dog, if trained when young. Siamese and Burmese cats are the easiest breeds to train. Some cats can be trained to follow their owner without a leash.

NEW CATS

Flat-faced cats may suffer from blocked tear ducts.

In nature, changes take place over a long period of time and become established only if they prove an advantage. When humans control breeding, natural forces are overridden. Domestic cats have not changed for thousands of years, but in the last century cats have been bred for their looks. A selection of extreme mutations has produced some breeds that can only survive as pets.

CURLY COAT
The Devon Rex, first discovered in the west of England, has a coat with few guard hairs, but a lot of curly down hairs. It sheds less fur than other cats. It has very big ears and eyes.

PEKE-FACED PERSIAN KITTEN
The characteristics of a Persian cat are a snub nose, a flat face, and long, silky fur. A new type of Persian cat is bred to have a face like a Pekinese dog. They sometimes develop breathing problems.

STUMPY TAIL

The Manx cat is named after the Isle of Man in the Irish Sea where it is believed it first appeared. It has no tail bones or only a few, so it has either no tail or a small stump.

ORIENTAL BEAUTY

The elegant Siamese has been bred for hundreds of years in Thailand. The dark colour "points" include face, ears, legs, paws, and tail. This cat has tabby-striped points. Siamese always have blue eyes.

Tabby points were introduced in Siamese cats by breeding with a tabby cat.

MUNCHKIN CAT

The Munchkin is a very recent American breed, named after the little people in *The Wizard of Oz*. It was bred from a short-legged cat discovered in Louisiana.

MALE LION

An adult African male lion is the only member of the cat family with a full mane. Even the Gir lions of India do not have full manes. Like bobcats, lynx, tigers, and some domestic cats, they have a ruff of long fur from their ears to beneath their chins.

FINE FURS

All cats have magnificent fur coats to protect them and keep them warm. A fur coat is made up of several kinds of hair. Guard hairs form a coarse outer coat. They can stand on end to make a cat look bigger. Thinner awn hairs with bristly tips provide an inner coat. Soft crinkly down hairs make an insulating undercoat. Cats living in cold climates have very thick fur.

Ear tufts are made of long dark hairs.

TUFTED EARS

Caracals, living in hot, dry areas, have long tufts of hair growing from the tips of their ears. Bobcats and lynx also have ear tufts, but live in far cooler climates. The purpose of the ear tufts is unknown.

WILDCAT FUR

A close-up view of the fur of a European wildcat shows the thick down hair that forms an insulating layer, trapping warm air near the skin. Long, glossy awn hairs cover the down hair. The tips of awn hairs form a protective coat that repels rain.

Long awn hairs

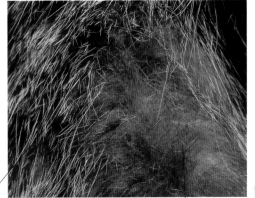

Down hairs

CHEETAH AND CUBS

Small cheetah cubs grow a long, fluffy, gray coat that makes them look like an aggressive animal called the honey badger. This may help to protect them from predators when their mother has gone hunting.

Fluffy gray coat

NORTHERN LYNX

These lynx live in remote forests in North America and Asia. In winter their coats become paler in colour. They grow furry breeches to keep their back legs warm. Their furry paws help to keep them from sinking in soft snow.

SPOTS AND STRIPES

Cats need camouflage to stalk and hunt. A tiger's stripes help it to blend into a back-ground of strong sunlight and shade. The lion's coat is the same colour as the dry grassy plains on which it lives, and a leopard's spots conceal it amid the shade of a leafy tree. Some jaguars and leopards living in forests have such dark coats that it is hard to see the spots on them. Sadly, most of the wild cats have been hunted for their beautiful coats.

HIDE AND SEEK

An adult lion hunts by stalking its prey. When a group of lionesses hunt together, they slink as close as possible to a herd of grazing animals. The lionesses' golden coats camouflage them in the long grass.

Some stripes have a spot of colour in the centre.

Tiger

Jaguar

TIGER AND JAGUAR

A jaguar's spots (left) are shaped like rosettes with central spots. Some spotted cats have circles and blobs, often in one colour. Tigers (far left) are striped. Domestic tabby cats can be striped and spotted.

THE LEOPARD'S TAIL

The fur underneath the tip of a leopard's tail is white. Female leopards often raise their tails so that the white fur shows as a "follow me" signal to their cubs.

BENGAL TIGER

These tigers live in dry forests, rain forests, and even bamboo forests and grassland. In all of theses habitats their striped fur looks like the long shadows cast by leaves. Tigers need their camouflage to hunt.

Tigers seem to vanish in dense forest.

GROWING LION CUB

Lion cubs are born with spotted coats. These disappear as the cubs get older, although sometimes the spots remain, especially on the lower parts of young adults. Many cubs and kittens have patterned coats to help camouflage them and protect them from predators.

CATS' EYES

Shine a light at a cat's eyes in the dark and they glow. This is because cats have a light-reflecting layer, called the tapetum lucidum, at the back of each eye to help them see in the dark. In bright sunlight the pupils of a cat's eyes contract, or get smaller, to protect the eyes from damage. Cats do not see colour as well as humans do. This makes it more difficult for them to pick out objects that are not moving.

NIGHT HUNTING
When a leopard hunts at night it opens the irises of its eyes as wide as possible to let in the maximum amount of light. All cats have good night vision. They need much less light than human beings do to see at night.

SHINING EYES
A cat's eyes appear to shine in the dark. In fact, light reflects back off the tapetum lucidum, the silvery layer at the back of each eye.

SMALL CIRCLES
In bright light, the pupils of a big cat's eyes contract to a small circle. In smaller cats, the pupils contract to a slit. Cats have good binocular vision for judging distance.

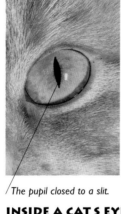

The pupil closed to a slit.

The pupil open wide.

A DOMESTIC CAT S EYE
The pupil, the dark centre of the eye, is surrounded by the iris, the coloured part of the eye. The iris opens and closes to control the amount of light let into the eye.

Eyes of different colours are often linked with white fur.

INSIDE A CAT S EYE
Cats' eyes are large, their eyeballs are rounder than ours, and the lens (which focuses the image) is set near the centre. This gives cats a wide angle of vision.

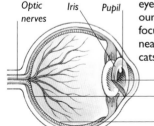

Optic nerves
Iris
Pupil
Lens
Tapetum lucidum
Retina

ODD EYES
Cats' eyes can be many colours, ranging from amber to green and blue. White cats with blue eyes are often deaf. If each of their eyes is a different colour, they are less likely to be deaf.

EARS AND WHISKERS

Cats have excellent hearing. They can pinpoint which direction a sound is coming from with the great accuracy. The slightest sound or movement will give away the position of its prey. Cats can detect high frequency sounds that humans cannot hear. They also have an acute sense of space because their whiskers are highly responsive to small changes in air pressure.

ANTENNAE

A serval's large ears are excellent at picking up sounds, and they can swivel to face most directions. A serval hunts in long grass and can follow the noises made by a small rodent underground. The serval pounces as the rodent leaves its burrow.

A cat has 24 whiskers, 12 on each side.

CURIOUS CAT

A cat's whiskers and eyebrows have nerve endings at their roots, making them very sensitive to touch.

CATS' WHISKERS

A cat can focus its whiskers backward and forward like antennae. The top two rows move independently from the bottom rows. They give the cat information about the shape and movements of its catch, so it knows how best to kill it.

A cat's whiskers bend forward as it jumps.

SHARP EARS

Most cats go hunting at dusk, or during the night. Good directional hearing is all-important for the night-hunter. It tells the cat exactly where to seek its prey in the dark. Cats move quietly on padded paws.

Whiskers "feel" around the space.

HOW BIG?

Whiskers are twice as thick as ordinary hairs, but so sensitive they are able to register the size of an opening without touching it. A cat knows automatically if there is enough room for it to get through.

SMELL

Smell is very important to cats. They use it to identify friends, mark their territory and recognize that of others, and to know when a female is ready to mate. Cats have several scent-producing glands. Family and friends rub each others' scent glands on cheeks, chins, and lips. They mark territory with their claws, urine, and feces. Cats hunt by sound and sight, not by following a scent trail, as some dogs do.

WELCOME GREETING
A cat rubbing against your legs may be welcoming you home. It is also finding out where you have been from the smells you have picked up, and rubbing its own scent on you.

In winter animals leave a trail of paw prints in the snow.

COLD NOSE
Scent-sensitive membranes cover a large area behind a cat's nose and provide a good sense of smell. Most cats do not rely on their noses when hunting. However, this European lynx appears to be sniffing tracks left recently in deep snow.

CATNIP
Most domestic cats love the smell of a plant called catmint or catnip. They roll on it to cover their fur with the scent.

The Jacobsen's organ is behind the upper teeth.

FLEHMING
Cats have a specialized organ for smell, the Jacobsen's organ. It is linked to the mouth by an opening behind the top teeth. This tiger is transferring scent particles with its tongue to this organ. This is called flehming. Cats flehm to detect the scent given off by cats that are ready to mate.

Some scent glands are found on a cat's lower cheeks.

MY MUM
Cubs and kittens rub their mother's face often to exchange their scent with hers. Cats, especially females living in groups, rub faces. The dominant cat receives more rubs than any of the others.

WASH AND BRUSH UP

To clean areas like the top of the head, which a cat cannot reach with its tongue, it dampens the back of a paw and wipes it over its fur. Tangles and burrs are carefully bitten out.

One paw goes over the head, around the ears and eyes, and down the nose. The other paw cleans the other side.

USEFUL TONGUE

A cat's tongue performs many useful jobs. It laps up water when a cat drinks. When a cat eats its prey the tongue scrapes flesh from bones with the sharp backward-pointing spikes that cover the centre of its tongue – cats do not have the right type of teeth for gnawing bones. A cat's tongue also plays a vital role as brush, comb, and washcloth in keeping its coat clean and tidy, and in helping it to groom other cats.

CHIN UP

Cats keep their kittens clean all over. The mother's rough tongue removes all dirt and combs the fur. Mother and cubs exchange licks and nuzzles whenever they are together.

SANDPAPER TONGUE

You feel how rough a cat's tongue is when a cat licks your hand. It is covered with spiked points that help it remove flesh from bones. Imagine what it would feel like to be licked by a lion! Its huge tongue is so rough that it can scrape off skin.

The tongue acts like a scraper.

A lioness and cub keep their eyes open for danger while drinking at a water hole.

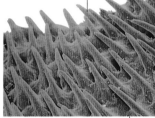

Papillae on a cat's tongue are hard and sharp.

SPIKY TONGUE

The top surface of a cat's tongue is covered with small, hard spikes, called papillae, that all point backward. When a cat licks itself, they work like bristles, brushing and smoothing the cat's fur.

THIRSTY LIONS

Some cats live in very dry areas. To drink, a cat's tongue curves to collect water, which it flicks back into the mouth. Cubs and kittens usually continue to suckle their mother long after they have begun to lap water.

29

TOOTH AND CLAW

CAT BITE
Using their pointed canine teeth, cats stab between their victim's backbones to cut its spinal cord. The spacing between the canine teeth differs between males and females, and between species. Each type of cat is an efficient killer of a different type of prey.

Retractable grasping claws are a cat's first weapon. Most cats use their claws to grip and hold their prey. It is important to kill quickly to avoid being hurt by a struggle. All cats have conical-shaped canine teeth. They are full of nerve endings; a cat will test-bite swiftly before delivering a deadly bite that severs its victim's spinal cord. Animals that are too large to be killed in this way are choked to death by a bite to the throat or muzzle.

Canine teeth

OLD SOLDIER
A male lion gains many battle scars. He may have to fight to gain control of a pride, and to defend his territory from other male takeovers. The hooves and horns of prey animals also inflict their share of injuries on the lion's face.

WEAPONS

A cat's claws are lethal weapons that can rip open an opponent. Even tiny kittens have sharp claws. Cats sharpen their claws by scratching off the blunt outer layer on a rough surface to reveal a new sharp claw.

FIGHTING

Cats only fight when the rewards are worth the risk of being injured. They fight to win territory or a mate. These cats are only pretending to fight as the cat on the left is bigger and older than the cat on the right.

BATTLING TIGERS

Tigers often box and wrestle as they fight violently. The weaker animal will usually concede defeat. Tigers are the biggest cats of all. Males can weigh 270 kg (600 lb). Tigresses also fight each other to secure their own territory.

Fighting tigers are very noisy.

A playful paw does not make contact.

A quick tumble leaves only the tail as a target.

CAT CALLS

Cats need to communicate with each other – a mother and her young, cats that live in large family groups, those few that live as couples, rival males, and cats looking for a mate. They meow, wail, growl, chirrup, squeak, cough, hiss, and purr. Only lions, tigers, leopards, and jaguars can roar. Cats also use body language and their expressive ears, eyes, and faces to signal their meaning. You do not have to be a cat to understand most of these expressions.

ROAR!
A lion roars to communicate with the rest of the pride and to show who is boss. An angry lion coughs with rage. A lioness calls her cubs with a soft mew and her mate with a low growl.

FRIENDLY GREETING
A confident cat walks straight ahead, its tail held high and curled slightly forward at the tip.

ADOPTING A POSE

A frightened cat hisses and growls. It arches its back and its hair stands on end, making it look bigger and more frightening. This kitten is is adopting a frightened pose during a boisterous game.

The vulnerable belly is exposed to signal defeat.

GAMES FOR LIFE

These young cheetahs are playing. One has rolled onto its back to expose its belly and show submission. The other keeps its ears flat, ready to fight. It stares its competitor in the eye to maintain its dominant position.

A frightened cat flattens its ears.

Wide open eyes

DOMESTIC QUARREL

A confident attacker walks tall and twists its head as it approaches a crouching rival. An aggressive cat that is not afraid keeps its ears low and twisted forward. This is a signal that it may attack at any moment.

A fluffy tail makes the attacking cat look bigger.

JUMPING AND LEAPING

Cats are muscular animals. Their hind legs are especially strong and work like powerful springs. A domestic cat can easily jump five times its own height. Leopards leap 3 m (10 ft) between rocks, and one was recorded jumping 6.6 m (22 ft) in a single leap. Cougars and lynx have very long hind legs. A cougar was once seen making an enormous leap of 12 m (40 ft) across a stony gorge.

The tail flexes in a curve as the cat leaps at full stretch.

A cat may use its claws to grip as it pushes off.

A cat uses its hind legs to spring into a jump.

JUMPING UP

When jumping up onto a wall or into a tree, a cat judges how high to jump by gauging the distance from the ground. It crouches, then springs upward. When it lands it is ready to move again at once.

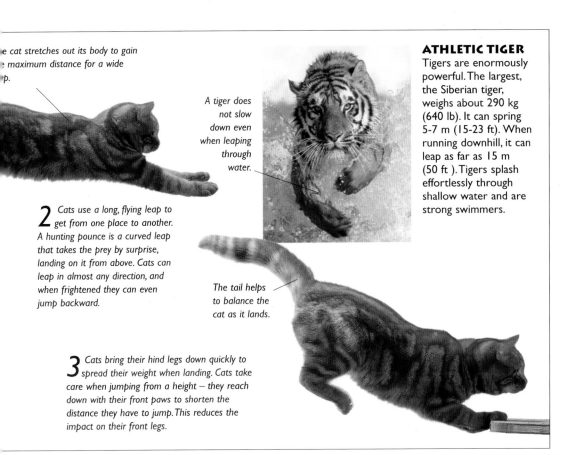

...e cat stretches out its body to gain ...e maximum distance for a wide ...p.

A tiger does not slow down even when leaping through water.

2 Cats use a long, flying leap to get from one place to another. A hunting pounce is a curved leap that takes the prey by surprise, landing on it from above. Cats can leap in almost any direction, and when frightened they can even jump backward.

The tail helps to balance the cat as it lands.

3 Cats bring their hind legs down quickly to spread their weight when landing. Cats take care when jumping from a height – they reach down with their front paws to shorten the distance they have to jump. This reduces the impact on their front legs.

ATHLETIC TIGER

Tigers are enormously powerful. The largest, the Siberian tiger, weighs about 290 kg (640 lb). It can spring 5-7 m (15-23 ft). When running downhill, it can leap as far as 15 m (50 ft). Tigers splash effortlessly through shallow water and are strong swimmers.

BALANCING ACT

Cats' claws make climbing easy. Leopards and some of the smaller cats spend much of their lives in trees, and domestic cats love a high viewpoint from which to survey their territory. All cats have an excellent sense of balance and can land feet-first if they fall. They have an organ inside each ear that signals to the brain so it knows the position of the body in the air. Cats also use their tails to help them balance.

CRITICAL BALANCE
Most domestic cats can walk along the narrowest of fences without falling. They place their paws one in front of the other. Their tails are used to counter-balance any wobbles.

WHAT GOES UP
Climbing is easy for this bobcat kitten, but coming down is much more difficult. Curved claws make it easier to come down backward, then jump when the ground is close enough.

FREE FALL

A falling cat always turns in mid air so that it lands on its feet. This remarkable manoeuver is accomplished by alternately stretching and retracting its fore and hind limbs while it twists its lithe body. The cat rights itself in a split second and lands unhurt.

A cat arches its back and stretches out its legs to help absorb the shock of landing.

RUNNING DOWN

The margay is a small South American wild-cat. It has such flexible ankles it can run straight down a tree trunk head-first. It can also spring 2.5 m (8 ft) from the ground into the branches of a tree if it is threatened.

Margays are equally agile on the floor of the rain forest.

TREE STORE

Leopards are skilled climbers. They are strong enough to carry dead prey heavier than themselves up into the branches of a tree, and store it out of the reach of scavengers such as lions, hyenas, and jackals.

Leopards rest during the day and hunt at night.

TIGER WATER

Tigers lie in pools to keep cool in the heat of the day. A family will often lie together in the same pool. Tigers are strong swimmers but many do not like splashing their faces and enter the water backward. The Java tiger, which may by now be extinct, was recorded swimming across water channels 5 km (8 miles) wide.

WET CATS

Most cats do not like getting wet, although they will dip a paw into water and even swim if they have to. However, some jaguars thrive in the hot, wet rain forests of South America. They are excellent swimmers, and catch river turtles and occasionally larger prey. Tigers also like water and cool off in shallow pools in hot weather. The fishing cat has partially webbed feet and lives on the banks of rivers and wetlands in southern Asia.

DINNER TIME!

Most domestic cats love watching fish in an aquarium. They may dip in a paw to flip a fish out. Kittens are often taught this skill by their mother. Domestic cats have been known to jump into rivers or the sea to catch fish.

QUICK DIP

The Turkish Van cat originally came from near Lake Van in Turkey, where cats swam from fishing boats. When this cat breed arrived in Europe it was called the swimming cat.

The fur of this cat is thick and soft and does not easily get wet.

FISHING CAT

This rare wild cat lives beside streams and swamps. It is a good swimmer, catching fish and frogs as well as land animals. It is extremely shy, and scientists have found it difficult to obtain much information.

The fishing cat spends its life beside water.

PADDLING PAWS

Cats swim like dogs, moving first the left paw and then the right paw underwater. Small cats only have short bursts of energy. They soon get tired and have to find a place to scramble out.

TERRITORIES

Cats that live by hunting need an area with enough prey in it to support them and, when necessary, a growing family. No cat likes to have its prey disturbed by another; but a few small cat species, which eat different prey, hunt the same territory. Big cats often have territories that overlap. If so, the smaller cats avoid the larger ones. Lions and tigers attack leopards. Lions also chase cheetahs and will kill their cubs if they find them.

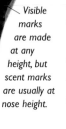

Visible marks are made at any height, but scent marks are usually at nose height.

TIGER SCRATCH
A tiger marks a tree by scoring it deeply. As well as leaving a visual sign, scratching also leaves scent marks from glands on its paws.

BLACK PANTHER
Panther is the name given to black leopards. Different cat species, such as panthers, can share a hunting territory if they seek different prey. The gape of the jaws varies in each species and is the right size for seizing a particular type of prey.

SCENT MARKING
All cats, male and female, mark territory by spraying urine. This leaves a scent message which identifies them and lets other cats know when they were there. Cats have regular spraying places and will place their markings on top of old ones.

WHOSE RIGHT OF WAY?
Many cats have territories that overlap, or they share certain routes that pass through each other's territory, such as a property wall. Cats can pass each other on neutral ground, but there may be a confrontation if one cat has to give way.

FARM CATS
Domestic cats who are feral (living wild) in towns often live as a group. Farm cats also form groups and share a territory, although each claims a small personal area. Pets in the same home also have to share a territory. There are three adult cats living in this barn. Apart from the mother with her kittens, two other cats are patrolling the tops of the internal walls.

Cats that use the same wall may spend time greeting each other.

STALKING TIGER

A tiger crouches under cover. It keeps its head and body down and runs forward taking its prey by surprize. It must get within 20 m (66 ft) of its prey before springing forward, because it cannot outrun most animals over a longer distance.

All cats are carnivores: they eat meat. Pet cats come when called to get their food, but wild cats have to find their prey and then catch it. Cats are highly specialized and skillful hunters that have adapted to many different environments. Some lie in wait for their prey and ambush it. Others creep as close as possible, then launch a surprise attack on their unsuspecting victim. Even cheetahs stalk their prey before starting a high-speed chase.

Rare white tigers have cream fur with brown stripes and blue eyes.

SURPRISE TACTICS

The serval hunts birds, rodents, and lizards. It locates its prey by listening hard to pinpoint its precise position. It springs clear of the grass and pounces on the unsuspecting prey from above.

BOBCAT STRIKE

A hare darts from side to side to escape the larger, slower bobcat. The bobcat stretches forward to swipe the hare's soft belly with its sharp claws. Hares often get away, and a bobcat has to be quick to kill its prey if it wants to eat.

KITTEN HUNT

Young kittens know instinctively how to stalk and pounce. Their mother shows them how to kill their prey quickly with a bite. If cats are not hungry, they often keep practicing or playing with a small victim.

The lioness grips a wildebeest with her strong paws while trying to bite its throat.

The hare leaps sideways to try to escape.

FAMILY FEAST

Lions and tigers can kill animals heavier than themselves. They use their large canine teeth to grip their victim's muzzle or throat and prevent it from breathing. Lionesses usually hunt in groups and will share the kill. They share with males, too.

PAIRING UP

This tiger's ears show that he is not making an aggressive approach.

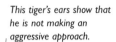

Few cats live in pairs, so most cats have to find a mate. Females signal when they are ready to mate by calling and marking a wide area with scent. They may select more than one male and continue mating for several days. Males usually compete among themselves to win females. The kittens of small cats are born 60-70 days after mating. The cubs of big cats may be born 119 days after mating. There is now evidence that some males some-times help a mother and her cubs.

TIGER TOGETHERNESS

A tiger starts his courtship cautiously. When the female accepts him, he begins a friendly greeting, rubbing his face against the female's and licking her. Mating takes place several times an hour and is a noisy affair with loud growls and snarls.

FLIRTING
A female cat that is ready to mate rolls around on the ground near the male.

GO AWAY!
A lion may be rejected when he first approaches a lioness. A lion may guard a lioness for days before and after he knows she is ready to mate, to try to prevent other lions from fathering her cubs.

LEAVE ME ALONE
After mating, a female cat often turns on the male and drives him away by hissing and striking him with her paws.

A FIRM GRIP
A lion gently bites a lioness on the scruff of her neck during mating. This grip seems to keep the lioness calm and submissive. Most cats mate in exactly the same way, usually making loud cat noises.

THE YOUNG

Kittens and cubs are born blind and helpless. A mother cat is careful to find a safe hideaway for their birth so that the new kittens and cubs can be kept hidden. Some mother cats move nest sites constantly to keep them secret and safe. Lionesses or domestic cats living together may feed each others' young, so the mother can go hunting. Mother cats feed, protect, play, and teach their young. When a mother is away hunting, cubs and kittens may be attacked and killed.

NEWBORN KITTEN

Kittens and cubs are born with their eyes closed. They do not open them for several days, and their vision is poor at first. However, scent and touch enable them to rapidly find their mother's nipples and begin suckling.

A mother's rough tongue acts as both washing cloth and hairbrush.

CLEANING BEHIND THE EARS

Cat mothers keep their cubs clean, licking their fur, eyes, ears, and bottoms. She also removes waste from the nest area.

DINNERTIME

The first milk that kittens and cubs get from their mother, known as colostrum, contains antibodies that protect them from infectious diseases. The cubs will knead a teat with their paws to increase the flow of milk.

TIME TO MOVE

When a nest site is endangered a mother carries her litter to a new one. This cat has gently grabbed a kitten in her jaws and is quickly carrying it to safety. The kitten is not hurt by its mother's teeth, and hangs quietly in her clasp without moving.

The kitten curls its legs clear of the ground.

COUGAR ON GUARD

Cat mothers are fiercely protective of their young. Left alone, kittens and cubs are unable to protect themselves. They do not attempt to help their mother chase intruders.

PLAY AND LEARN

Kittens and cubs learn the skills they will need as adults by playing with each other and with their mother. They practice stalking, chasing, pouncing, and fighting. When the cubs of big cats are about six months old, they follow their mother on hunting trips and watch her hunting technique. They learn about her territory and how prey behave. A mother cat may bring back live prey for her young to kill. Many cubs and kittens do not survive their first year.

A low-profile stalk

BABY BOB
This bobcat kitten has to learn to be a skillful hunter in winter, when temperatures fall below freezing and food is scarce.

LION CUBS

A parent's flicking tail is a fascinating toy – fortunately adult lions are very patient with their cubs. The cubs learn to be reasonably gentle when they bite and bat at their parents. The roughest games are played with other cubs.

BOUNCING CHEETAHS

Each litter of cheetah cubs has a unique pattern of spots on their tails. Male litters of cubs often stay together for life. They will defend a territory together, but hunt alone. Playing together strengthens the bonds between brothers but most adult cheetahs live alone. Cubs are looked after and fed by their mother until they are old enough to fend for themselves.

Cheetah cubs leap and bounce around.

A kitten crouch, ready to spring forward in a game of pounce.

LEARNING TO HUNT

A kitten's toys are leaves, balls of string, or anything that moves and can be stalked and chased. It will use these skills when hunting as an adult.

PROUD FATHER

Male lions defend the pride's territory and protect the females and cubs. They are driven away when new males succeed in taking over the pride. Newcomers usually kill existing cubs to make the females mate with them.

Males are very tolerant of their own cubs.

FAMILY PRIDE

Most lions live in family groups called prides. The lionesses do most of the hunting. They frequently work as a team, surrounding a grazing herd and selecting one animal to chase. Sometimes they drive their prey into an ambush. The leading lioness checks that the others are in position before springing an attack. Female cubs stay in their mother's pride, but male cubs move to find a new pride when they are mature.

SHARED PARENTING

Females in a pride share in suckling and rearing young cubs. The lioness leaves the pride to give birth and usually returns when the cubs are old enough to follow her safely. A few leave to form a new pride.

FAMILY PRIDE

The size of a pride varies according to the territory and quantity of prey. In India, a pride may be only two males and three or four females. In Kenya, prides of five males and twenty lionesses are known. There are eleven females and older cubs in this pride. The lions are not resting with them.

Large prey can be hunted most successfully by a team.

Young lions learn by watching their parents. Young males may form a bachelor group before joining a new pride.

FIRST SHARE

Lions in a pride leave most of the hunting to the females, but they get a share of food. When food is short it is the cubs who go without. If cubs die, lionesses breed when food becomes plentiful again.

Males feed first if they are near a kill.

TEAM HUNTING

Lions hunt at all times of the day but are most successful at night, especially when there is no cover. One pride has learned a trick to kill buffalo: the largest lion holds the buffalo's tail while the others attack its throat.

ANDEAN CAT

This cat lives above the snowline in the Andes, the mountain chain in South America. It hunts for chinchilla and other rodents. It is officially recognized as an endangered species and is protected in Peru.

VANISHING CATS

Almost all cats, except domestic cats, are rapidly declining in numbers. Cats have long been hunted for their fur coats, or because they kill farm animals, or for sport as "big game." Some cats have become extinct during this century, and other species are now endangered. Today the habitat of many wild cats is destroyed and cleared for timber or farmland. Some cats are still victims of the fur trade, even where this is illegal. The Bengal tiger may not survive in the wild beyond the next ten years.

Long soft fur keeps the cat warm.

GEOFFREY S CAT
This South American cat lives in forests and scrubland. The population of the Geoffrey's cat is being dramatically reduced by fur trappers.

HIDING IN SCOTLAND
In the past, Scottish wildcats were hunted for their striped fur. More recently, they were exterminated by gamekeepers protecting young game birds. Once common throughout Scotland, wildcats only survive in isolated places today.

BLACK-FOOTED CAT
This tiny wildcat of southern Africa weighs only 1 kg (2.2 lb). It lives in dry grassland and deserts. It is very rare and only survives in remote parts of the Kalahari Desert.

ENDANGERED TIGERS
The Java and Bali tigers are extinct and other tigers are endangered. An Indian government program to protect the Bengal tiger has failed to deter poachers.

53

INDEX

Leopard

*Stalking
kitten*

Jaguar and cub

Curious cat

Mother and kitten